A Topic for Everyone

Women's Group Discussion Topics and Activities

Also By Pat Brill and Karen Fusco

Essentials for Starting a Women's Group

(Currently available in paperback at Amazon.com,
on Kindle, and as an e-book at www.womens-group.net)

Busy Moms: The Heart and Soul of a Home

(Currently available on Kindle and as an e-book at
www.busymombook.com,
soon to be available in print at Amazon.com)

A Topic for Everyone

Women's Group Discussion Topics and Activities

Pat Brill and Karen Fusco

A Topic for Everyone

Published in the United States of America by Boomers In Motion, LLC.

For more information, contact the publisher at:
Boomers In Motion, LLC
213-37 39th Avenue, #314
Bayside, NY 11361
(877) 574-5526
info@boomersinmotion.com

Additional paperback copies may be obtained at Amazon.com or as an e-book on Kindle.

ISBN: 978-0-9833442-5-4

Table of Contents

The Topic is the Topic 1

Selecting a Topic 2

Topic Phobia 2

Topic Themes 3

Women's Group List of Topics 5

Business/Work—Discussion Topics 5

Charity—Discussion Topics 7

Charity—Activities 8

Entertainment—Discussion Topics 10

Entertainment—Activities 11

Feedback—Activities.........................13

Field Trips—Activities.........................14

Finance—Discussion Topics....................16

Goals—Discussion Topics 18

Group Names—Discussion Topics 20

Health—Discussion Topics 21

Learning—Discussion Topics 23

Learning—Activities 25

Legal—Discussion Topics....................26

Let's Get Physical—Discussion Topics....................27

Let's Get Physical—Activities 28

Outside Speakers or Services—Activities....................29

Parenting—Discussion Topics 31

People Focus—Discussion Topics 34

TABLE OF CONTENTS

Personality—Discussion Topics 36

Personality—Activities 37

Powerful Questions—Discussion Topics 38

Roles—Discussion Topics 41

Self-Awareness—Discussion Topics 43

Self-Help—Discussion Topics 45

Self-Help—Activities 48

Spiritual/Religion—Discussion Topics 51

Spiritual/Religion—Activities 53

About the Authors **55**

II

The Topic is the Topic

Are you the Visionary who's decided to start her own women's group and wants to be well prepared ahead of time? Are you a member of an already established women's group that needs some new ideas to stimulate great discussions?

Now is the time to concentrate on what you will talk about at each meeting. This is known as the Featured Topic. Having a strong and thought-provoking Featured Topic will make your meeting all the more productive for every member.

Karen and Pat, the authors of "Essentials for Starting a Women's Group" have put together a fabulous list of possible Discussion Topics and Activities for you and your women's group to use. It is by no means a complete list and is meant to help get your juices going.

A number of these ideas came from members in our women's community, Women's Group Busy Bites, who are currently participating in a women's group of their own. They are from all around the world. Visit www.womensgroupbusybites.com to check it out.

We're sure you'll be able to find other topics and activities we've never even envisioned – and they'll likely be more relevant to you and your group. Until inspiration hits you or you've run out of your own great ideas, use our ideas to begin your discussions.

Selecting a Topic

When selecting a Featured Topic, consider the stated focus or theme of your women's group, the type of members you're appealing to and even the time of year.

Some groups are very general in nature, concentrating on self-growth or expanding one's horizons, for example. This opens up almost any topic as a possibility. If your group has a more focused theme, your list of topics may not be as broad, but it will no doubt delve more deeply into the group's specific areas of interest.

Topic Phobia

When you rotate the choosing of a topic between all members of your group, you will find that not all members are equally comfortable with finding an interesting topic.

Some members find coming up with topics very easy. They have an endless supply of creative ideas and fabulous topics at hand with hardly any thought at all. They draw from their daily lives, their activities and their dreams.

Others suffer at the mere thought that it's their turn. "Why can't I come up with a good topic?" is a common question. Anxiety takes over. There's a fear associated with putting oneself out there in this way. What if no one likes my topic? What if it bombs? What if it's boring? There are lots of what-if's.

Having this book at hand for your group members will certainly help them to choose a successful topic and ease their anxiety.

We have actually found some of the topics we groaned about the most ended up to be wonderful experiences, leading our discussions to places we'd never visited before. Stay open and learn.

Topic Themes

For groups that meet often – say once a week – and have a specific focus, it may be a good idea to have one theme for an entire month. It may be easier for your members to come up with overlapping or related topics to be presented in successive meetings.

At the start of a new month, your group can select a topic theme to cover all meetings that will occur during the month.

The Topic is the Topic

Then, at each meeting, a different subject falling under that theme can be chosen by the member who's in charge of picking the topic.

Using topic themes to cover multiple meetings can be an interesting thing to try out. If it works for your group and allows for delving into specific areas, keep it going. If your group prefers constant variety, let the topic selection be open to each member's creativity.

Women's Group List of Topics

Business/Work—Discussion Topics

▶ Building a network of support among your co-workers

▶ Find your perfect job

▶ For service professionals – Learn to care for yourself so you are able to care for others

▶ Help business women build their dreams and feel good about themselves

▶ Home based working moms

▶ How friends became business partners

▶ How many careers have you had? Are you where you want to be in five, ten, fifteen years?

▶ How to deal with a difficult co-worker

▶ If you had the choice to retire right now, would you? What would you do in your retirement?

▶ Keeping up with technology in the work place

▶ Live with passion – Do what you love

▶ Managing the stress of work and home

▶ Managing your boss

- ▶ Pearls of great worth (building creative leadership)
- ▶ Pros and cons of close friendships in the workplace
- ▶ Pros and cons of working vs. homemaking
- ▶ Roles of men vs. women in the workplace
- ▶ Self-employment – the challenges and benefits of owning one's own business
- ▶ The well balanced life – Should you bring your work home with you?
- ▶ What job would you do if you could have any job in the world?
- ▶ What's been your funniest/weirdest job title?
- ▶ Your workspace style – what it is and how to get it

Create your own list of
Business/Work related Topics and Activities

_____

_____

_____

_____

_____

_____

_____

Charity—Discussion Topics

▶ Brainstorm ways to give back to your community

▶ Choosing a charitable organization to support and making sure your values line up with theirs

▶ Finding time – small ways to give back

▶ Large charitable organizations vs. small organizations

▶ Personal benefits of participating in volunteer work

▶ What good can one person do in the grand scheme of things?

▶ When enough is enough – How much should you give both of your time and your money/resources?

Charity—Activities

▶ Ask members to bring specific items for a battered women's shelter to each meeting

▶ Blood drives which include a full breakfast

▶ Book drive – Send books to low income schools around the US.

▶ Can drive or Food drive to support local food cupboards

▶ Clothing drive

▶ Make sandwiches for a homeless shelter. Each woman brings a loaf of bread and sandwich makings. Making and wrapping sandwiches allows for talking and sharing for hours.

▶ Organizations to support from UK: Dogs Trust, Barn Bow Lassies, the W.A.A.F.

▶ Silent auction where you donate the proceeds to a local group

▶ The value of giving back – Check your local women's refuge or battered shelter. Ask if they need something that would be useful and inexpensive. Then go about fulfilling that need either within your group or host a drive to accomplish it.

▶ Toy drive during the holidays

▶ Teen night – Get your women together and offer an activity for teens in your area. It could be anything from an all night party to a movie night.

▶ Volunteering as a group or as individuals – Groups who seek volunteers:

- Libraries – story hour, stocking shelves, cleaning, organizing
- Schools – tutoring, bus help, after school programs
- Churches – food cupboards, kids programs and activities, cleaning
- **Organizations** – Red Cross, Salvation Army, ASPCA, YMCA, Community aides: most communities have one or more organizations to help those in need right in your own community

**Create your own list of
Charity related Topics and Activities**

_____

_____

_____

_____

_____

_____

Entertainment—Discussion Topics

▶ Discuss a movie you recently all watched

▶ Movie ratings

▶ Music – the appropriateness or inappropriateness of
_____ (fill in musician/album)

▶ The evolution of music

▶ The evolution of television

▶ What's your favorite book and why?

▶ Story telling:

- What's one mischievous thing you did when you were a kid that you never got caught doing?

- What's one mischievous thing you did that you regret?

- What's one thing you wish you'd have done when you were a kid/teen?

- What was the best Christmas present you ever received and why?

Entertainment—Activities

▶ A birthday sleepover

- Send husband (and kids) away for overnight, bring in food, watch movies and celebrate together

- Go away overnight anywhere to celebrate a great occasion

▶ A group garage sale

▶ Attend a local play, show or concert

▶ Birthday celebrations – go out to lunch or dinner together to celebrate another member's birthday and everyone treats the birthday girl

▶ Board game night

▶ Bunco night ice breaker – It's a fun game which forces players to change partners each round thus encouraging socialization within the group

▶ Christmas party/buffet with party games

▶ Comedy club

▶ Crafting night

▶ Create a list of fun outings that members enjoy doing together

▶ Design and create note cards or holiday cards as a group

- ▶ Have a women's Super Bowl Sunday gathering – If you're not into football and it's big in your area, have your own fun day while the men are otherwise occupied.

- ▶ Karaoke

- ▶ Overnight shopping trip

- ▶ Pot luck dinner

- ▶ Quiz night – possibly a music night quiz with all sorts of questions covering pop, jazz and classical

- ▶ Traveling / picnic ideas

- ▶ Video game night – Find someone in your group who owns a Wii or a similar game system. You'd be surprised how much fun the adult generation can have with it!

- ▶ Wine tastings

**Create your own list of
Entertainment related Topics and Activities**

_____

_____

_____

_____

_____

_____

Feedback—Activities

We all crave feedback from others, so here are some ideas that could be welcomed in your group.

▶ Each member writes on an individual sheet of paper the name of each of the other members. Next to each letter of the person's name, write a word that best describes that individual. This is anonymous and all answers can be read aloud at the end.

▶ Have a suggestion box for discussion topics or general changes/ideas for the group.

▶ Write one thing you like about each person in the group (anonymously), fold it up and put the person's name outside. Take turns reading other people's statements. This is an encouraging activity. The individuals don't know who thought what about them, yet everyone will leave the evening feeling really good about themselves.

**Create your own list of
Feedback related Topics and Activities**

_____

_____

_____

_____

13

Field Trips—Activities

Take a group "field trip" to add a new element to your women's group. Whether it's for learning a new skill, hearing a speaker, engaging with the arts or simply getting out for a fun excursion, it'll add some spice to your group and draw your members closer to each other.

▶ Antiquing

▶ Arts & Crafts exhibition

▶ Attend a lecture

▶ Attend local seasonal festivals

▶ Go to a movie and use that as the focus of your next group

▶ John Edwards or other uplifting speakers

▶ Line dancing, country dancing

▶ Museum trip/Art gallery

▶ See a concert, ballet, show, play

▶ Support the youth in your community by attending their school concerts, drama productions and musicals

▶ Walking tour in your community

▶ Walking tour of your nearby large city

▶ Wine tasting tour

▶ Zoo trip – Yes, these are still for adults

Create your own list of
Field Trips related Topics and Activities

_____

_____

_____

_____

_____

_____

_____

_____

_____

_____

_____

_____

Finance—Discussion Topics

▶ Bargain hunting – sharing our best secrets

▶ Financial literacy

- This could be good for outside speakers

- If you have someone in your group that has the 'knowledge,' then let them present a topic and discussion meeting

- Create a list of financial areas you want to know more about

▶ How much money would you need to be happy?

▶ How to save for vacations – Treat them as a necessity, not a luxury

▶ How to stay within budget during the holidays

▶ Looking good on a budget

▶ Money: mine, his and ours

▶ Setting up the right budget for you

▶ Stock market – Have those members who are more knowledgeable provide information in this area so all can learn and benefit

▶ What would you do if you won $1 million dollars today? Would you spend it? How?

▶ What's your belief about money? Do you believe it is the "root of all evil?" Do you have positive or negative feelings associated with money?

Create your own list of
Finance related Topics and Activities

_____

_____

_____

_____

_____

_____

_____

_____

_____

_____

_____

Goals—Discussion Topics

▶ 10 things to accomplish within a year – Write them down. Have someone hold them for a year and then look back at them a year later.

▶ A goal you set that you have yet to accomplish

▶ A previous goal you set and how you accomplished it

▶ Clutter control

▶ Create an exciting vision of what's possible

▶ Hopes and dreams for the future

▶ How to create meaningful goals

▶ If you had all the time in the world, what would you do?

▶ New year's resolutions (keep and read the following year)

▶ Reconnect to your passions

▶ Setting a relationship goal – Marriage, troubled friendship/family relationship

▶ Setting goals for your children

▶ Short term vs. Long term goals

▶ The ultimate New Year's resolution: doing nothing

▶ Value clarification and goal setting

Create your own list of
Goals related Topics and Activities

_____

_____

_____

_____

_____

_____

_____

_____

_____

_____

_____

Group Names—Discussion Topics

- ▶ Create a group motto
- ▶ Create a group tag line
- ▶ Create an identity for your group, a logo, letterhead, etc.
- ▶ Find a theme for your group and a name that describes it well

**Create your own list of
Group Names related Topics and Activities**

_____

_____

_____

_____

_____

_____

_____

_____

_____

Health—Discussion Topics

▶ Dieting – what works, what doesn't

▶ Doctors vs. Alternative Therapies

▶ Exercise – Outdoor/Indoor, Summer/Winter

▶ Healthy eating for adults

▶ Healthy eating for children

▶ Healthy eating for teens

▶ Herbs and seeds – How can we benefit by adding them to our lives?

▶ How to have quality of life when you have an illness

▶ How to have quality of life when someone you love is ill

▶ Making sure you have "you" time

▶ Meditation/prayer benefits on your health

▶ Menopause – many topics here!

▶ Nutrition – topics around different types of nutrition. This also a great topic to bring a speaker in.

▶ Old wives tales – Do they work for you?

▶ Reducing stress – Stress impacts your physical and emotional well-being. Perfect for brainstorming on how to reduce stress in our lives.

▶ Self-healing – In what ways can you heal yourself?

▶ Wellness and healing – It is essential that women know how to handle stress in a productive healthy way. It is also imperative that we know how to recognize symptoms of stress and how to heal this issue on all levels.

▶ What do you do for relaxation?

▶ What do you do for fun?

▶ What do you do for excitement?

▶ What is your body telling you right now? Do you feel good in your skin or uncomfortable?

▶ Woman's health issues – this topic was a favorite for many members of our community

**Create your own list of
Health related Topics and Activities**

_____

_____

_____

_____

_____

_____

_____

Learning—Discussion Topics

▶ Are we too old or too rusty to learn something new?

▶ Conflict resolution exercises

▶ Do you prefer giving advice or getting advice? Why?

▶ Gossip. How is it helpful? Harmful?

▶ How can you learn to forgive others? And forget? And move on when you don't really want to?

▶ How can you learn to forgive yourself?

▶ How can we each look at the world with a positive attitude?

▶ How do you like to be creative?

▶ How do you take in information?

▶ Are you a visual learner?

▶ A book-reading learner?

▶ An auditory learner?

▶ How to be a good listener

▶ If you could teach three things to others, what would they be?

▶ Should you go back to school?

▶ What are you reading?

▶ What can we do to learn how to communicate better?

LEARNING

- ▶ What have you always wanted to learn (or do) but have never managed to do it?

- ▶ Did you not have the time?

- ▶ No money available?

- ▶ Were you afraid of the challenge?

- ▶ What have you most recently experienced for the first time in your life?

- ▶ What is your learning style – visual, auditory, or kinesthetic?

- ▶ What new subjects or hobbies do you want to learn and add to your life?

- ▶ What role does music/art/dance play in your life?

- ▶ What role does trust play in your life?

- ▶ Your personal recipe for ... health, happiness, success

Learning—Activities

▶ Attend a play or concert together

▶ Study hypnosis

▶ Take a course as a group – art class, line dancing, cooking, etc.

▶ Take field trips to a museum or special collection.

▶ Teach the group – Each member can spend a week teaching the group one thing – a craft, recipe, game, skill

▶ Visit historical homes or sites in your area – and do some wine tasting while you're there!

**Create your own list of
Learning related Topics and Activities**

_____

_____

_____

_____

_____

_____

_____

Legal—Discussion Topics

▶ Completing your wills – Why and what is important in creating your will?

▶ Insurance – What do we have and what do we need?

▶ Learn about wills, powers of attorney and other necessary legal documents to protect yourself and your family

▶ The value or validity of a pre-nuptial agreement – Should you have one?

▶ Turn your group into a DBA or LLC or charitable entity – Learn the rules and regulations

**Create your own list of
Legal related Topics and Activities**

_____

_____

_____

_____

_____

_____

_____

Let's Get Physical—Discussion Topics

▶ Cycling, hiking, traveling, dancing – How to support each other in creating space for physical activity in our lives

▶ Keeping it sexy – always keep your diva status, go to bed sexy, wake up sexy, go to work sexy (not revealing), go to the store sexy

▶ Putting forth your best physical self, even at home

▶ Sex – Come on, you know you want to talk about it!

▶ Secrets – sharing helpful tips for ladies

• Some women in your group may deal with physical problems like corns, acne, allergies, thinning hair and the like. They may have some secrets on how to deal with these physical issues that will benefit all the members in your group.

Let's Get Physical—Activities

- ▶ Country line dancing – No partners are needed and they often teach you how to do specific dances
- ▶ Exercise classes of various kinds (tai chi, dance)
- ▶ Go for walks together. Have a picnic along the way
- ▶ Join a gym – You might even get a group membership discount
- ▶ Yoga or tai chi sessions – with lunch or dinner and sharing the bond of physical health together

Create your own list of
Let's Get Physical related Topics and Activities

_____

_____

_____

_____

_____

_____

_____

Outside Speakers or Services—Activities

▶ Bring in someone who could add value to your women's group. Find those in the community who are interested in women's growth in addition to their specialty.

▶ Fortunes told using tarot cards

▶ Have a make-up artist come to your meeting and give each of you a facial makeover. For example, Mary Kay representatives will come to a home.

▶ Massage – Have a massage therapist come to your meeting to give a 20 minute massage to any interested member while the others discuss a related topic.

▶ Mindfulness and relaxation – Bring someone in to teach 'mindfulness meditation' and share the experience together of adding emotional and physical wellbeing to your lives.

▶ Personal makeovers

▶ Speaker: Feng Shui your house, your work space, your room

**Create your own list of
Outside Speakers or Services related Topics and Activities**

_____

_____

_____

_____

_____

_____

_____

_____

_____

_____

_____

_____

_____

_____

_____

Parenting—Discussion Topics

▶ Adult children – How to build a different relationship with your adult children

▶ Be a parent, not a friend

▶ Children, children, children – This is a broad topic and you can survey your members to see what areas around children they are interested in discussing.

▶ Dealing with teenagers

▶ Extra-curricular activities – How involved should your child be?

▶ Fun outings for children

▶ Healthy eating for kids – ways to include healthy foods in their diet

▶ How can spirituality affect your family's health?

▶ How to talk to your children about (inappropriate) "touching"

▶ Letting your children grow up in the increasingly dangerous society that we live in

▶ Mealtime conversation – Make sure everyone at the table is included in the conversation at meal time. And, make sure that no one hogs the floor all the time.

▶ "More than a Mother" – Balancing this role with other important parts of your life

▶ Organizing back-to-school for your children

- ▶ Play dates for moms – important to set up time to be with other women without the children

- ▶ Rainy day ideas with children

- ▶ Should your child do chores without being paid?

- ▶ Spanking as a form of discipline

- ▶ To vaccinate your children or not

- ▶ Transition from working woman to new mom and the emotions that come with it

- ▶ Travel with kids – Research and come up with creative ways to relax while on vacation with kids.

- ▶ What are the five most important values you want to give to your children?

- ▶ What is important when you communicate and how can you become a better communicator?

- ▶ What is your parenting style? Do some research around different parenting styles and discuss what works or doesn't work for you with your particular style.

- ▶ What makes a great mother?

- ▶ What do you do when you and your spouse disagree about child rearing? How can you learn to come together on these issues?

Create your own list of
Parenting related Topics and Activities

_____

_____

_____

_____

_____

_____

_____

_____

_____

_____

_____

_____

_____

_____

_____

People Focus—Discussion Topics

▶ Always there for you – Do you have someone who cares, or are you the person who gives without receiving back?

▶ Dealing with the death of a loved one

▶ Divorce

    • Is it a correct solution to a difficult relationship

    • Is it a cop out?

▶ Do you play games or manipulate others? How does that help you or interfere in your relationships?

▶ Forming healthy relationships

▶ Friendship/best friend – Do you treasure your friendships?

▶ How can you make your couple time special? Try adding "dates" back into your daily life.

▶ How do you give back to your family?

▶ How do you give back to your community?

▶ How do you give back to the world?

▶ Ill or dying parents – Provide support, suggestions and solutions to help a member deal with older parents

▶ Listening – What are your strengths and weaknesses when listening to yourself and others?

► Male and female relationships – How are they different for each of you?

► Social connections – What type of social connections do you have in your life? Are you enhancing those connections?

► The friendship that wasn't – Dealing with the loss of a friendship through anger or difficult circumstances

► Two are better than one – Is that true?

► What issues arise when you feel unsupported by yourself and/or others?

► What relationships in your life have been the most fulfilling?

► What relationships in your life have been the most troubling?

Create your own list of
People Focus related Topics and Activities

_____

_____

_____

_____

_____

_____

Personality—Discussion Topics

▶ Are you happy with your personality?

▶ Are you a perfectionist? How does it help or hinder you?

▶ Do opposites really attract each other or are they really the same type of people wrapped up in different styles of interacting?

▶ Does your personality get in the way with others?

▶ Has your personality changed over the years?

▶ How do extroverts and introverts work together? Or do they?

▶ What is your personality type?

▶ What personality types bother you?

Personality—Activities

▶ Studying and categorizing personality types in various ways

- Type A/Type B
- Sanguine/Melancholy/Phlegmatic/Choleric
- Introvert/Extrovert
- Sensing/Intuitive
- Thinking/Feeling
- Judging/Perceiving
- http://www.personalitypage.com/high-level.html
- http://en.wikipedia.org/wiki/Four_Temperaments

▶ Take a personality test

**Create your own list of
Personality related Topics and Activities**

_____

_____

_____

_____

_____

37

Powerful Questions—Discussion Topics

▶ Are you a risk taker? How has that helped or hindered you in your life?

▶ Are your habits controlling you? Which habits work for you and which habits do not?

▶ Describe your perfect life. Remember it is perfect in every way. What do you feel, hear, taste, touch and see?

▶ How are you your own worst critic?

▶ How can you free yourself from old stories or patterns that hold you back?

▶ How do you celebrate yourself?

▶ How do you get beyond bad decisions you've made in the past?

▶ How do you keep track of your memories? Do you write, take pictures, movies, etc?

▶ How has your life differed from what you dreamed about as a child?

▶ How important are animals in your life? If they are important, why? How do they add to your life and help you be the person you are today?

▶ How would you like people to describe you if you died today?

▶ If you could interview any famous woman, who would it be? What would you ask her?

▶ If you could live anywhere, where would that be?

▶ Is your home set up to support you?

▶ What are the five things you are most proud of about yourself and why?

▶ What are your five most important values you want to live by? How do you incorporate them into your life?

▶ What book or film has impacted you a lot recently and why?

▶ What do you think your life has been about?

▶ Morality

　• What does morality mean to you?

　• How do you live by your own morality? Or don't you?

▶ What dreams of yours have come true?

▶ What happens to you when you face a challenge? Do you shrink from it? Do you jump in and attack the problem?

▶ What historical figure(s), dead or alive, do you admire? Why?

▶ What is one thing you regret doing/one thing you regret NOT doing?

▶ What is your legacy?

▶ What life lessons have you learned? How will you pass them on?

▶ What personal figures, dead or alive, do you admire? Why?

▶ What were the best five years of your life and why?

▶ Where are you currently in your life?

▶ What comes next?

▶ Where have you been and where are you going?

**Create your own list of
Powerful Questions related Topics and Activities**

_____

_____

_____

_____

_____

_____

_____

_____

_____

Roles—Discussion Topics

▶ Balancing all of your relationships. This is a very powerful subject because all of you have to deal with the many roles you have in your lives, and you have to add yourselves to the mix.

• Friends

• Spouse

• Family

▶ How to keep your marriage lovely forever

▶ If you could choose, in your next life, what or whom would you be?

▶ If you were a flower, what would you be? And why?

▶ If you were an animal, what would you be? And why?

▶ Role playing activities

▶ Romantic treasures

▶ Share romantic ideas or romance enrichment products.

▶ How do you romanticize your bedroom for your husband, just because? Candle-light, balloons, rose petals, a card, wine, soft music, etc.

▶ Sister Circle – Learn how to support each other in times of trouble

▶ The various roles of a woman – wife, lover, sister, friend, mother, daughter, grandmother etc.

- ▶ The working mother

- ▶ The working woman

- ▶ To work or not to work? A very important question for moms.

- ▶ We know you take care of others. What do you do to take care of yourself?

- ▶ What does it mean to be a woman? Who defined this for you?

- ▶ When did you know you were an adult?

**Create your own list of
Roles related Topics and Activities**

_____

_____

_____

_____

_____

_____

_____

_____

_____

Self-Awareness—Discussion Topics

▶ Are your weaknesses really important?

▶ Be yourself – Are you yourself? If not, why not? If so, what do you do to be yourself?

▶ Decision making: Are you good at it? What are tools for making good decisions? Do you hesitate, waver or jump right in?

▶ Do you seem to repeat the same patterns (or mistakes) over and over? How can you change that?

▶ How are you controlled by your appearance?

▶ How are you controlled by your weight?

▶ How do you engage in negative self-talk?

▶ Identify your level of satisfaction in various aspects of your life

▶ Make choices – don't just go along. When do you make choices and when do you generally follow the choices of others? Does it work for you?

▶ Share three things you hate about yourself

▶ Share three things you love about yourself

▶ What are your problem solving skills and what are you lacking?

▶ What are your strengths and weaknesses?

▶ What excites you the most in the world?

► What is your greatest achievement?

► What was the happiest moment in your life? How did you feel? How did you experience it?

► What was your best (or favorite) decade? Why? What did you accomplish or experience?

► Are you stuck in a rut? How do you extricate yourself?

**Create your own list of
Self-Awareness related Topics and Activities**

_____

_____

_____

_____

_____

_____

_____

_____

_____

_____

Self-Help—Discussion Topics

▶ Acceptance – start with yourself

▶ Affirmations – Do you believe it works?

▶ Are you superficial or deep?

▶ Ask each person what they will do for 'fun for one hour a week', just for themselves and how they will implement it

▶ Assertiveness – How does it help or hinder you in your daily life?

▶ Be thankful for all the wonderful things you have in your life today. What are they?

▶ Describe how fear affects you. Choose any word to replace fear (disappointment, anxiety, stress, etc).

▶ Do you think of yourself as powerful? How so?

▶ Emotional intelligence – identifying and managing emotions

▶ Enjoy your journey – What ways can you celebrate or show gratitude for your current path in life?

▶ Forgiveness – Is forgiveness part of your life?

▶ Forgiveness – What are the benefits?

▶ Gratitude – How do you create space for gratitude in your life?

▶ How can you build more compassion towards yourself? We can easily give compassion to others but feel uncomfortable about giving it to ourselves.

▶ How do you remember to take care of you each day? And how does your family support or not support you in this endeavor?

▶ How does negativity impact you in your life?

▶ How to be your own valentine

▶ How to find joy in everyday living

▶ Learn to love yourself first, then you can love others

▶ Life changes – changes we experience and changes we wish to experience

▶ Move on – How do you help yourself move forward in your life?

▶ 'One of the silliest things you have done!' – Only those who are happy to share need to join in. Great for a belly laugh and to just relax and learn to laugh at yourselves.

▶ Personal grooming tips

▶ Procrastination – How has it affected your life? What can you do to stop procrastinating?

▶ Ritual vs. Habit – How do you know the difference?

▶ Self-development – Is self-development part of your life?

▶ Self-empowerment – How can you develop confidence in your own capacity?

▶ Take a personal issue and find fun and creative ideas to resolve it

▶ Time out – the importance of taking time out for yourself and ideas on how to spend the time for yourself, on yourself

▶ Unconditional love – Is there such a thing called unconditional love?

▶ Ways to take care of yourself

▶ Ways you can add extreme self-care into your life

▶ What are the benefits of journal writing? How does one do it?

▶ What does change mean to you? Are you afraid of change? Why?

▶ What fears/obstacles have you overcome in your life?

▶ What inspires you?

▶ What makes your heart sing?

▶ What type of magazines do you read and why? How do they fulfill you?

▶ When do you make choices and where do you generally go along with things or others? Does it work for you?

Self-Help—Activities

▶ Breathing exercises

▶ Bring magazines and cut out words that describe you or are important in your life

▶ Book study – Choose a book to study with your group. Use it as a basis for discussion.

▶ Design a family crest

▶ Design and make a group quilt

▶ Gratitude – For the creative part of the evening make a gratitude journal

▶ Great gift ideas – A wonderful brainstorming activity as many get blocked with this topic. Get a large pad and list all the key people you buy for. Then brainstorm creative and unique gifts for them over some drinks or nibbles.

▶ If you could only describe yourself in pictures – Gather magazines and cut out the images that define and describe you

▶ Learn and practice tapping exercises – Known as EFT, tapping uses the ancient principles of Chinese acupuncture to address your feelings (especially the negative feelings) about issues you experience on a regular basis

▶ Meditation

▶ Start a group scrapbook

▶ Vision boards – Create a pictorial board around what you want to include in your life. Gather magazines and cut out images and words to capture how you want your life to be. Make a collage of them all on your personal vision board.

▶ Visualization exercises

▶ Write your epitaph

▶ Yoga class

▶ Your beliefs – Get a piece of paper and on one side list one positive belief you have about yourself. On the other side list one negative belief you have about yourself. Below each, list five pieces of evidence that prove the positive belief to be true and five pieces that prove the negative belief is false.

**Create your own list of
Self-Help related Topics and Activities
(we left lots of space for these!)**

_____

_____

_____

_____

_____

_____

_____

_____

_____

_____

_____

_____

_____

_____

_____

_____

_____

_____

_____

_____

_____

_____

_____

_____

_____

Spiritual/Religion—Discussion Topics

▶ Are you more spiritual or rational?

    • Are these opposites?

    • Could you benefit by adding more of the other trait?

▶ Book of Esther – focusing on this book from the bible

▶ Brokenness – focus is to create spiritual recovery

▶ Faith in the workplace

▶ How can spirituality affect your family's health?

▶ How can spirituality affect your relationships with others?

▶ How to build a spiritual home

▶ Metaphysical group for women – opening our minds and becoming more spiritual

▶ Power in prayer – This subject is good for all walks of life. You can fast together or pray for specific reasons.

▶ Pursuing your destiny

▶ Sharing your faith with others

▶ Spirituality

    • What does it mean to you?

    • Where are you in your spiritual quest?

    • Do you feel you are spiritual?

- ▶ The blessing of Christian fellowship
- ▶ The Holy Spirit – building a relationship with your maker and reaping it's benefits
- ▶ What are your underlying spiritual beliefs?
- ▶ What does it mean "to feed my sheep?"
- ▶ What is your divine purpose?

Spiritual/Religion—Activities

▶ Bring your minister in to speak to the group

▶ Faith suppers – A Potluck meal: a gathering of people where each person contributes a dish of food to be shared among the group

▶ Meditation – add value to one's spiritual focus as well as maintaining one's health

▶ Past lives regression – Refer to Michael Weiss regression tapes as an example of how to do this

**Create your own list of
Spiritual/Religion related Topics and Activities**

_____

_____

_____

_____

_____

_____

_____

_____

_____

About the Authors

Karen Fusco, a mom with two grown daughters, owns Creative Solutions, where she designs and writes custom software, and Creative Properties to manage her real estate holdings. She is also a Busy Mom Expert®.

Pat Brill, a mom with a grown son and daughter, owns Prime Bookkeeping, where she provides small businesses with bookkeeping and human resources services and she founded The Women's Group.

Together Pat and Karen own Boomers In Motion, LLC, the parent company for all their internet ventures.

They have been active members of The Women's Group since 1997.

For more information about women's groups and women's issues, visit our blog at:
http://www.WomensGroupBusyBites.com

You can also follow us at:
http://www.facebook.com/womensgroups
http://www.twitter.com/womens_groups

or email us at:
info@womensgroupbusybites.com

ISBN: 978-0-9833442-5-4

Made in the USA
Middletown, DE
18 March 2020